Crows are large, bold, noisy birds. You will know the 'croak' and 'caw' they make, and you will have seen flocks of them in fields on cold winter days or on their own in the garden.

There are many types of black crows: carrion crows, ravens, rooks and jackdaws. They are mainly black; only some crows have a grey-and-black coat. Magpies and jays also belong to the crow family.

Ravens are the biggest crow, with a great wing-span and a long bill. They tend to live alone. Rooks have pale faces, nest in a big colony and feed in the open.

Crows eat most things: seeds, nuts, crops, frogs, eggs, insects, mice and voles. They peck at the bones of carrion (which means dead animals) on the road.

Crows chase off those birds of prey that get close
to their nests and don't stop till they go away.
This is called 'mobbing'.

Crows are very clever. Some crows pick up sticks
in their beaks and poke them in holes to get at
bugs. Jackdaws drop stones into a pond to raise
the water level so they can drink.

You can train pet jackdaws to do tricks and to say things. Both crows and jackdaws can remember a face and know to stay away from mean people.

Do you know the phrase 'Stone the crows!'? You can say it when you are shocked. It is from the days when it was common to throw stones at crows to stop them eating seeds in the fields.